For Ray, who loves them all,
great and small

— L.G.-B.

To my parents,
Barbara and Walter

— A.G.

What is the difference between
a frog and a toad?

Is that a moose or a caribou crossing the road?

• Both frogs and toads are amphibians.

• A frog's skin is thin, smooth, and moist.

• Most toads have thick, rough, dry, and bumpy skin. The bumps may look like warts, but touching a toad will not give you warts.

• Frogs can leap twenty times their body length with their strong back legs.

• Frogs never go far from damp places.

• Slugs and snails are the favorite foods of some frogs. Others use their sticky tongues to catch insects.

• Some frogs protect themselves by changing color to match their surroundings.

• Toads have broad bodies and short legs. They do not jump like frogs but make short hops or walk.

• Most toads live on land, where it's drier.

• Toads like to feast on ants. A toad can eat as many as three hundred ants at one sitting!

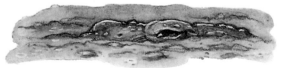

• To avoid their enemies, toads burrow into the ground, play dead, or even puff up.

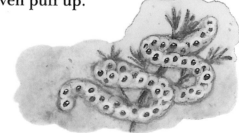

• Frogs and toads both go into the water to breed and lay eggs every spring.

• The moose, the largest member of the deer family in North America, has dark brown fur and weighs up to eighteen hundred pounds. Moose have large ears, a broad, overhanging lip, and a tassel of hairy skin at the throat, called a "bell."

8-9 feet tall

• Only male moose have antlers. Moose antlers are broad and flat like the palm of the hand, and have up to forty points in a rack.

• Moose live alone or in small family groups. In warm months, they wade in lakes and rivers, eating water plants.

• Like cow hooves, moose hooves are split in the front, so moose can walk on marshy ground.

• Caribou are smaller deer, weighing around five hundred pounds. They are dark brown like moose but have a distinguishing white neck and rump. Caribou have short ears and no overhanging lip or bell.

4-7 feet tall

• Both male and female caribou have antlers. Caribou antlers are smaller than moose antlers and are curved instead of flat.

• Caribou graze on the tundra in large groups, eating plants and grasses. Up to ten thousand animals travel together during fall and spring migrations.

• Caribou have large, wide, rounded hooves with patches of hair on the undersides. With these snowshoe-like hooves, they move easily across spongy tundra or snow and ice.

Is that a dolphin or
a porpoise making the playful,
diving leap?

Is that an octopus or a squid
swimming down in the deep?

• Dolphins and porpoises are small whales that live in the ocean. They are not fish but marine mammals. Female mammals nurse their young with milk. There is a fish called dolphin. Plentiful in U.S. waters off Hawaii and the East Coast, this dolphin is often referred to as *mahi-mahi*, Hawaiian for "dolphin," when sold commercially.

• A dolphin's snout is very pointed. In fact, the dolphin's entire body is longer and more streamlined than the porpoise's.

Bottle-Nosed Dolphin 10-14 ft.

• Porpoises have blunt snouts and broad, rounded flippers. Their back fins are small and square.

Harbor Porpoise 4½-6 ft.

• Dolphins have been known to swim alongside ships and boats. Highly intelligent animals, they also perform tricks in oceanariums. Flipper is a dolphin.

• Most porpoises avoid contact with ships and are not trained to do tricks like dolphins are.

• Dophins prefer to feed on shrimp.

• Dolphins often swim under schools of yellowfin tuna. Fishermen netting these tuna watch for leaping dolphins. When the tuna nets are drawn in, however, many dolphins are often trapped because they cannot reach the surface to breathe. They eventually drown in the net.

• Porpoises eat fish like herring and sardines.

- Both squid and octopuses are ocean dwellers.

- An octopus has a round body and eight arms, or tentacles.

- A squid's body is long and tapered, with ten tentacles. Eight are short, and two are longer and thinner.

- Some kinds of octopuses grow up to thirty feet across, but most are much smaller.

- Many species of squid are less than a foot long, but the giant squid may be over fifty feet long.

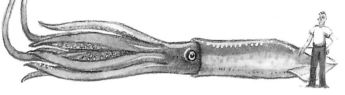

- Octopuses usually stay in shallow beds close to shore.

- Squid live deep in the open ocean.

- Octopuses can swim, but they usually crawl. Each arm is lined with tiny suction pads, which help them to grip when moving from place to place.

- Most squid are strong, fast swimmers.

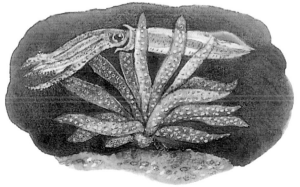

- Female octopuses guard and clean their eggs.

- Female squid do not guard their eggs.

- Both octopuses and squid use the sucking discs on their arms to capture fish and crabs.

- When octopuses or squid are frightened, they squirt a black liquid into the water. They hide from their enemies behind this inky smoke screen.

What's the difference between
a snail and a slug?

Is a spider the same as a bug?

• Snails and slugs have long, soft bodies that are shaped like tongues.

• Snails and slugs both have two tentacles, with an eye mounted at the end of each. They both have a muscular foot, which they use to pull themselves along on their stomachs.

• Snails and slugs eat plants. Slugs damage garden plants and crops. Snails do not.

• Snails have hard, spiral-shaped shells on their backs. Like turtles, they can withdraw their bodies inside these shells for protection.

• Most slugs do not have a protective shell.

• Slugs secrete mucus from a gland near their heads. Along this wet, slimy trail slugs can move easily over dry surfaces. Did you ever see the ribboning white lines made by a slug on the sidewalk? Snails do not leave this mucous trail.

• Snails live on land, in fresh water, and in oceans. One land snail, the escargot, is cooked and eaten.

• Most slugs live in woods, fields, and gardens. Sea slugs live in rocky pools and shallow water.

• There are many kinds of insects. True bugs are one order, or kind.

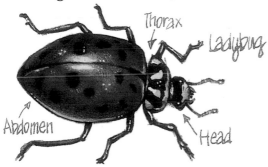

Thorax
Ladybug
Abdomen
Head

• Like other insects, a true bug's body is divided into three parts.

Beetle Fly Wasp

• These bugs have antennae, and most have two pairs of wings, and can fly.

• True bugs cannot make silk or spin webs.

• Most true bugs do not trap prey. They use their long, piercing, sucking mouths to drink juices from plants.

Elephant Stag Beetle

• Most true bugs have a scent gland that discourages animals from eating them.

Stinkbug

• True bugs can be harmful to plants and people. Stinkbugs destroy garden crops, and chinch bugs damage grainfields. Bedbugs suck blood from people.

Colorado Potato Beetle

• Insects have six legs. Spiders have eight legs, so they are not insects.

Black and Yellow Argiope
Abdomen
Cephalothorax

• Spiders' bodies consist of two parts.
• Spiders have no wings or antennae.

• Some spiders trap insects, like flies, mosquitoes, and moths. After injecting the insects with an enzyme that liquefies their insides, the spiders suck the liquid, leaving the empty skin behind.
• Spiders do not have scent glands.
• Spiders help humans by trapping harmful insects. Spiders in England and Wales alone kill 200 trillion insects annually.
• Web-spinning spiders have liquid protein in their abdomens, which comes out through spinnerets. This liquid hardens into strong silk strands sometimes only a millionth of an inch thick. In a one-acre meadow, spiders can spin enough silk in a week to surround the moon, a distance of 6782.5 miles.

zowie!

Is that a beaver or a muskrat
gnawing at the log?

How are a swamp
and a marsh different
from a bog?

• Both beavers and muskrats are gnawing rodents.

• Beavers have broad, horizontally flattened tails shaped like paddles. When threatened, a swimming beaver slaps its tail hard on the surface before diving under the water. Slap!

• A beaver's head is squarer than a muskrat's.

• With their sharp teeth, beavers cut down trees like poplars and alders to dam up streams and form ponds.

• Strict vegetarians, beavers eat only the inner bark of trees and water plants.

Beaver Chips

• A beaver divides its time between land and water.

• The beaver is active mostly at dusk and in the dark.

• The beaver's lodge is built of branches and mud and has an underwater entrance.

• The smaller muskrat has a long, vertically flattened tail, which it moves back and forth like a rudder when swimming.

• Muskrats do not dam up streams or cut down trees.

• Muskrats eat cattail roots, swamp plants, and sometimes mussels and fish.

• A muskrat spends most of its time in the water.

• The muskrat is active almost all day.

• Some muskrats live in burrows along the banks. Others build houses of reeds in shallow marshes, with at least one underwater entrance.

• Swamps, marshes, and bogs are all wetlands. Wetlands are areas other than lakes or rivers that are covered with water for some part of the year.

• Water runs through a swamp. The soil in a swamp is shallow with a thin layer of minerals on top.

• Water also flows through a marsh. A marsh is rich in minerals because the soil's bacteria quickly break down plant and animal matter. Of the three types of wetlands, marshes have the richest plant and animal life.

• Water collects in, but does not run through, a bog. A bog may look dry, but it is actually spongy-wet. Without running water, acids in the bogs are not flushed out. The bog's surface is covered with rotting layers of plants called peat moss.

Egret

Sphagnum Moss

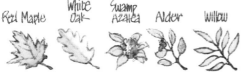

Red Maple White Oak Swamp Azalea Alder Willow

• Dominant plants in a swamp are trees and shrubs, which grow year-round. Most common are silver and red maple, swamp white oak, swamp azalea, alder, and willow.

• Plants in a marsh grow back each year. There are few, if any, trees or shrubs. Typical plants include orchids, water lilies, cattail, and arrowhead.

Water Lilies

Cattail

Arrowhead

• With few mineral nutrients, bogs have little plant variety. Acid-loving plants, such as black spruce, pitcher plant, cedar trees, and shrubs like bog laurel and cranberry, flourish.

Black Spruce   Cedar   Bog Laurel   Cranberry

• Similar animals live in both swamps and marshes. These include frogs, turtles, herons and bitterns, raccoon, beavers, wood ducks, and alligators.

• Fewer animals can live in bogs—mostly amphibians like frogs and salamanders.

Pitcher Plant

Leopard Frog   Spotted Salamander   Wood Duck

Which is the rabbit
and which is the hare?

Is that a butterfly or
a moth flying in the air?

• Hares have long legs and long ears. When alarmed, they jump high into the air. Jackrabbits, which are hares, can leap to twenty feet.

• Rabbits have shorter ears and legs. When alarmed, they run fast instead of jumping.

• Newborn hares are fully furred and their eyes are open.

• To protect themselves from their enemies, snowshoe, or varying, hares change color from brown in the summer to white in the winter. Their wide, furry, snowshoe-shaped feet prevent them from sinking into deep snowdrifts.

• Hares nest in piles of brush or in existing burrows. They do not dig their own burrows.

• Baby rabbits are born with no fur and closed eyes.

• Rabbits do not change color with the seasons. Their narrow feet are not designed for deep snow.

• Rabbits often dig burrows or use brambles and brush for nesting.

• Both hares and rabbits eat grasses, buds, soft plants, and tree bark.

• Both butterflies and moths have two antennae on their heads, which they use for smelling and feeling.

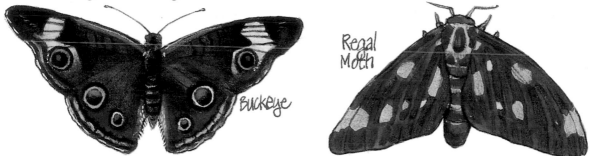

Buckeye

Regal Moth

• The wings and often the bodies of both butterflies and moths are covered with dustlike scales, which come off as a fine powder when touched.

• Both butterflies and moths have four life stages: egg, caterpillar, chrysalis, and adult.

1. Eggs   2. Caterpillar   3. Chrysalis   4. Adult

• Butterflies have smooth antennae with knoblike clubs at the tips.

• The body of a butterfly is thin and hairless.

• Most butterflies have large, brightly colored wings.

• Butterflies are active during the day.

• When a butterfly rests, it holds its wings upright over its back.

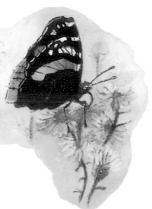

• Moths have feathery antennae with no clubs at the ends.

• A moth's body is generally fatter and covered with fine hairs.

• Moths have smaller wings that are usually dull.

• Most moths fly at dusk and at night.

• A resting moth stretches its wings out flat or wraps them around its body.

Is that an eagle or a falcon
carrying off a snake?

Is that an alligator or a crocodile
crawling toward the lake?

- Hawks are birds that eat other animals and are active during the day.

- Eagles are the largest hawks, with a wingtip span of six to eight feet. Bald eagles are not bald at all but have snowy white feathers on their heads.

- Bald eagles are usually seen near water, hunting for fish and waterbirds.

- Bald eagles soar into the air, riding the thermals.

- Because fish is the bald eagle's principal food, the eagles nest close to water, high in trees, in twig nests.

- Falcons are among the smallest hawks, with long tails and pointed wings. The kestrel is a colorful falcon with a cinnamon-colored breast and two black, mustache-like marks on its head.

- Kestrels perch on utility wires along roads or in trees as they search for rodents, snakes, and small birds.

- Kestrels seldom soar, but hover over fields while hunting for food.

- Kestrels nest in holes in trees, cliffs, or barns.

• Both alligators and crocodiles are reptiles—animals whose bodies are usually covered with scales.

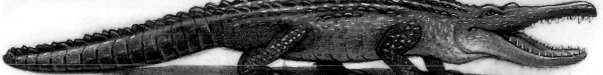

• Both alligators and crocodiles have enlarged fourth teeth in their lower jaws.

• Alligators, the largest reptiles in North America, grow up to twelve feet long.

• Crocodiles are smaller and thinner, and move faster than alligators.

• The alligator's snout is broad.

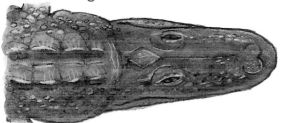

• The crocodile's snout is narrow and more pointed.

• Alligators do not have raised nostrils.

• The alligator does not have a toothy, "bulldog" smile because its bottom teeth do not stick out.

• Crocodiles have raised nostrils so they can breathe while underwater.

• The crocodile's lower teeth stick out when its jaw is closed, giving it a "bulldog" smile.

• Alligators rarely attack humans.

• Alligators live in freshwater lakes, swamps, and slow-moving streams.

• Saltwater crocodiles and Nile crocodiles are known as man-eaters.

• Nearly all crocodiles live in tropical salt marshes. Some species swim out into the open ocean.

Are those swarming insects
wasps or bees?

What's the difference between
deciduous and evergreen trees?

• A bee's short, stubby body is covered with fine hairs.

• All bees have stiff hairs on their legs, called pollen baskets. Bees collect and carry fine pollen dust from plants in these baskets.

• Bees lick or suck a sweet liquid from plants called nectar. They make honey from this sweet liquid.

• Bees and wasps that live and nest alone are called solitary. Those that live in large groups are called social bees and wasps.

Worker

Pollen

Nectar

Egg Pupae

• Social honeybees build wax honeycombs with hundreds of six-sided cells. In the honeycomb are chambers for young bees and for storing extra food.

• A wasp's body is tapered and smooth.

• Wasps do not have pollen baskets and do not pollinate plants.

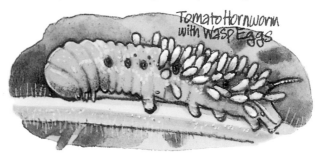

• Wasps have mouths that can bite. They eat meat, especially caterpillars.

Tomato Hornworm with Wasp Eggs

• The solitary female potter wasp builds a nest shaped like a tiny vase. She kneads clay with her front legs and then adds water.

• Social bees and wasps will sting anyone who comes near their nests. Solitary bees and wasps only sting when touched.

• Trees that lose their leaves in the fall are called deciduous, from the Latin word *decidere*, meaning "to fall off."

Red Maple

• Nearly all deciduous trees have large, broad, paperlike leaves, in one or several sections.

Shagbark Hickory

Elm

• Deciduous trees reproduce when insects pollinate their flowers. Some flowers are large and showy like the magnolia tree's. Others are hardly noticeable, like the oak tree's.

White Oak

Magnolia

• Leaves on deciduous trees live only about six months.

• Before deciduous leaves die, many display bright colors. These leaves always contain red or yellow pigments. But the chlorophyll that keeps the leaves green masks those pigment colors in warm months. In fall, days are shorter, so chlorophyll production slows down, letting the bright pigments emerge. Cold nights cause sugar to collect in the leaves, making the colors even more brilliant.

Sugar Maple

White Oak

Quaking Aspen

• Trees that stay green all winter are called evergreens.

White Pine

• Most evergreen leaves, called needles, are tough, thin, and coated with wax to help them survive hard winters.

Red Cedar

• Evergreen trees reproduce when wind blows pollen from their small pollen cones and lands on the scales of what will become the seed cones.

Norway Spruce

White Pine

Pitch Pine

Red Cedar

Red Pine

Hemlock

Juniper

Bald cypress

• Evergreen leaves fall off when they die, but some leaves of certain fir trees remain for seven years.

Is that a duck or a goose
walking in the rain?

What's the difference between a tornado and a hurricane?

• Geese are about twice as large as ducks. One familiar goose, the Canada goose, grows up to forty-five inches long.

• Geese have long necks and stout bills.

• Geese swim on the surface of the water, feeding on pondweeds and grasses. They do not dive for food.

• Geese often walk on land and eat grasses.

• All geese, including the Canada goose, fly together in large flocks of up to two hundred at a time during southerly fall and northerly spring migrations.

• Some geese have knobby bumps on top of their heads.

• A typical-sized duck is the hooded merganser, which is about eighteen inches long.

• A duck's neck is shorter than a goose's and its bill more slender and flat.

• Some ducks feed at the water's surface. Others, like the hooded merganser, dive under the water to catch fish and frogs to eat.

• Ducks spend most of their time in the water.

• Ducks fly alone or in small formations.

• Ducks do not have these head knobs.

• Both hurricanes and tornadoes develop when the air pressure drops.

• Tornadoes usually occur overland, especially in spring and early summer.
A tornado that moves over water is called a waterspout.

• A tornado forms when fast-moving, cold, dry air overtakes moist, warm air and the warm air twists upward. This twist is shaped like a funnel. Dust and debris are sucked into the funnel when it hits the ground. Tornado winds may spin up to 350 miles an hour.

• Destruction from tornadoes is caused by violent winds. Buildings are blown down or twisted apart.

• Meteorologists cannot predict a tornado's path because it develops with so little warning.

• Hurricanes occur in late summer and fall, and start over oceans that are at least 80 degrees Fahrenheit. Hurricanes strike coastal areas and lose power when they travel inland.

• In a hurricane, winds grow around a calm center of low pressure called the eye of the hurricane. These violent winds blow at least 75 miles an hour, usually accompanied by rain, thunder, and lightning.

• Much of a hurricane's damage is due to strong winds, heavy rains, high waves, and flooding along the ocean shore.

• Equipped with weather instruments, United States Air Force planes fly directly into the eye of a hurricane to locate the storm center and measure wind intensity. Meteorologists, people who study weather patterns, forecast a hurricane's path based on this data.

What's the difference between a
ring-necked pheasant and a ruffed grouse?

Which is the vole
and which is the mouse?

• The ring-necked pheasant is sleek and has a long, pointed tail. Males are colorful, while females have drab, buff-black feathers with shorter tails.

• The male pheasant has a dark, glossy, iridescent head and brilliant red eye patches. The bird gets its name from its showy white neck ring.

• Pheasant eat corn, wheat, and barley, often damaging farmers' grainfields.

• The pheasant lives around open farmland and at the edges of woods.

• The ring-necked pheasant makes a nest of dead leaves and grass, on the ground in fields.

• The ruffed grouse is shaped like a chicken. Both males and females have gray and reddish brown feathers, and fan-shaped tails.

• The grouse is called ruffed because of the males' ability to raise their neck feathers into a ruff when alarmed. During courting, the beating and drumming of grouse wings sounds like an engine starting up.

• Grouse feed primarily on the leaves, buds, and fruits of woodland plants.

• The grouse is only found in the deep woods.

• The ruffed grouse builds a shallow nest lined with leaves, in thickets or under logs.

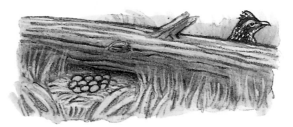

• Both voles and mice are mammals. They have fur, bear live young, and nurse their babies with milk. Voles and mice are also rodents. All rodents gnaw with their four large front teeth.

• Voles have short tails and small ears.

• Mice have large ears and a long tail.

• Mice have shorter fur.

• Voles have long fur.

• Most mice eat seeds and plants. One exception is the grasshopper mouse, which eats grasshoppers and other insects.

• Voles eat grass, grain, or most any plant. In winter, they strip bark off young trees, often killing them.

• Newborn voles can care for themselves at two weeks old.

• Baby mice are helpless for the first month of their lives.

• Voles build nests of shredded grass on the open ground. They have more young than any other rodents, bearing up to seventeen litters a year.

• Most mice build tightly woven, grassy nests under rocks, in logs, or in trees. They also hollow out nests in the walls of buildings.

Is that big black bird a raven or a crow?

What's the difference between hail, sleet, and snow?

- Crows and ravens are large black birds in the crow family.

- Crows are smaller, at nineteen inches long.

- In flight, most crows' tails are fanned out and squared.

- Crows gather in roosts with several thousand other crows.

- Crows have as many as twenty-three different calls. One of them is the common *cawcaw*.

- Crows live in cities, suburbs, farmlands, and woods.

Caw! Caw!

- Crows most often build nests in trees.

- Although crows prefer to eat corn, their diet also includes insects, frogs, and roadkills.

- The twenty-five-inch-long raven has a wingspan up to four feet. Ravens weigh four times as much as crows.

- In flight, ravens' tails are long and wedge-shaped.

- Ravens are more solitary and usually do not roost in large groups.

- Ravens have up to thirty calls, some of them a variation of *quork, quork*. A raven's voice is raspy and sounds a little like a crow with a sore throat.

Quyoorrk!

- Most ravens live deep in the northern forests, far from cities.

- Ravens usually nest on cliff ledges, although they may build their nest of sticks in large trees.

- Ravens feed primarily on dead animals, especially deer, but will occasionally kill small birds and frogs.

• All precipitation — a warm summer shower or a snowy blizzard — begins the same way. Water vapor cools and, after attaching itself to tiny dust particles, becomes either liquid or ice crystals. How the precipitation reaches earth depends on the temperature, the humidity, and how the air moves in the space between the clouds and the ground.

• Hail forms during thunderstorms in thunderclouds and is most common in the summer.

• The air in a thundercloud is freezing at the top and warmer at the bottom. Ice crystals form high in the cloud, then melt in warmer air. If air currents push the water drops back up, they freeze again. Continued bouncing up and down causes more water droplets to freeze onto an ice pellet and to grow.

• When the updrafts in the air currents aren't strong enough to keep the ice pellets in the clouds, they fall and hit the ground as hailstones. One of the biggest hailstones on record was seventeen inches around.

• Sleet is basically frozen raindrops. Sleet forms when snow crystals fall into a warm layer of air and melt.

These raindrops then hit freezing air again close to the ground and freeze. The newly formed ice pellets bounce as they hit the ground. Sleet feels like tiny, sharp needles on your face.

• Snow forms in cold weather when water vapor turns directly into ice crystals.

• Ice crystals cluster together and enlarge as they fall to the earth and land as snowflakes. The shape of snow crystals depends on the temperature and humidity of the air in the cloud in which they formed.

• Most ice crystals have six sides and exist in an endless variety of forms. A recent classification identified eighty different kinds, among them needles, columns, hollow prisms, and hexagonal plates.

Is that a bird or a bat
in the early evening sky?

Is that a tortoise or a turtle crawling by?

• Bats are the only mammals that truly fly. They are hairy, give birth to their young, and nurse their babies with milk.

• Bats have a thin stretch of skin connecting their long fingers to their hind legs, which acts as wings.

• With their small eyes, bats can see little at night. As they fly  bats send out high-pitched sounds that people cannot hear. These sounds bounce off objects and come back to the bats. The flying mammals use these sound waves to find food and avoid hitting things.

• Bats rest during the day, hanging upside down in sheltered places like caves and house attics.  At dusk, they dart about, catching insects on their wings.

• As insect-eaters, bats are helpful to people. One bat can eat as many as five hundred insects an hour. Some bats eat fruit, and others eat fish.

• Bats do not build nests. They roost in barns, caves, attics, and along cliffs. Mother bats often carry their young with them in flight.

• Birds, which are covered with feathers, are not mammals. Young hatch from eggs and are fed insects by the adults.

• Birds have good eyesight and do not give off high-pitched sounds like the ones bats make.

Great Horned Owl

• Birds are active during the day. One exception is the night-flying swift. At night, it can be difficult to tell a swooping swift from a bat.

• Birds build nests of many different materials. Swifts nest in wells, hollow trees, or chimneys. They glue their bark-and-twig nests with bird saliva, which hardens when dry.

- Turtles and tortoises are both reptiles that lay their eggs on land.

- Both turtles and tortoises have long life spans. Tortoises kept as pets live the longest of all. The longest-lived tortoise was documented at nearly two hundred years old when it died in 1918 on Mauritius Island in the Indian Ocean.

- Both turtles and tortoises have hard shells that protect their bodies.

- All tortoises and turtles can withdraw their heads and feet into their shells.

- The turtle's shell is flatter and more streamlined.

- Turtles have longer legs that are shaped like paddles. Unlike the tortoise, the turtle's toes are joined together by webbing. This makes it easier for turtles to swim through the water.

- Most turtles grow to be larger than tortoises. For example, green turtles weigh as much as nine hundred pounds, while giant tortoises grow up to six hundred pounds.

- Turtles live both on land and in water.

- Sea turtles can swim almost twenty miles an hour.

- A tortoise shell has a high, domed shape.

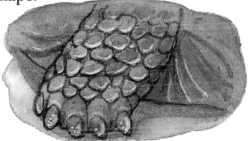

- Tortoises have heavy, short, club-shaped legs and feet. Their toes are short and not webbed.

- Tortoises live only on land.

- Most tortoises move very slowly. The top speed of the desert tortoise is well under a half-mile per hour.

Sigh...

INDEX